THE
Briefest
English
Grammar
AND
Punctuation
Guide Ever!

RUTH COLMAN grew up in a northern Sydney beach suburb and attended state schools. She did a colourful BA at the University of Sydney, and taught English at secondary schools for about ten years in Australia and Southeast Asia. Then she got sidetracked into editorial work, but still enjoys occasional ESL teaching.

A NewSouth book

Published by
NewSouth Publishing
University of New South Wales Press Ltd
University of New South Wales
Sydney NSW 2052
AUSTRALIA
https://unsw.press/

 A catalogue record for this
book is available from the
National Library of Australia

ISBN   9781742237954 (paperback)
         9781742238678 (ebook)
         9781742239613 (ePDF)

Internal design Josephine Pajor-Markus
Cover design George Saad

THE Briefest English Grammar AND Punctuation Guide Ever!

Ruth Colman

NEWSOUTH

Contents

PART 1: Grammar

PART 2: Punctuation

PART 1

Grammar

Preface to the grammar guide

When English speakers begin to learn other languages they often find themselves being taught via methods that assume they have a basic knowledge of English grammar.

Some of us, however, have come through a school system that taught little or nothing of the way our language is structured. We recognise when things 'sound right' or 'sound wrong' but we cannot say why. We now want to study a second language, to read it or speak it or both, and we are nonplussed when the teacher says, 'In German the verb comes at the end of the clause', or 'That's the indirect object.'

I hope this small guide will fill a gap and give you the basics, whether you want to learn another language or not, and if you do, whether your aimed-for second language is Spanish, Anindilyakwa, New Testament Greek, Swahili or anything else.

Don't forget that many languages don't have direct equivalents of all our classes of words or all our grammatical structures. Some systems of grammar are simpler than the English system, some are more complex, and some are simply different.

 **Intro**

How do we identify and classify words and groups of words? Whatever the language, it's a matter of function.

When people want to speak, they need ways of . . .	**In English we call these words . . .**
• indicating things and people	nouns and pronouns
• talking about actions	verbs
• describing things	adjectives
• describing actions	adverbs
• showing how things relate to other things	prepositions
• joining sections of speech	conjunctions

Quite often there is overlap. Words don't always fit neatly into the categories we think they should be in. Sometimes a group of words performs the function of one word, and some words have more than one function. But by and large the outlines in this book cover most situations. As you go through it you will find new meanings for some common English words – which simply indicates that grammar has its jargon just like any other field of study.

Sentences

Sentences are groups of words that make complete sense. When you give me a sentence I know you have told me or asked me something complete.

Sentences can be short . . .

- *Anwar lives there.*
- *Where are you going?*

or longer.

- *Sedimentary rocks, wherever they are, tell us about ancient climatic conditions, and geological events that happened in the area during the time the sediments were deposited.*

Sentences can be statements . . .

- *Susan hasn't paid her rent for two months.*
- *All these toys were made by Uncle Joe.*

or questions . . .

- *Are you well?*
- *Have they finished painting the house?*

or commands.

- *Come to the office at ten.*
- *Stop!*

Here's an exercise
(the only one in the book).

Which of the following are sentences and which are not? Can you tell why? Full stops and capitals have been omitted.

- the house on the hill
- he's finished the story
- in the cupboard
- but whenever we see him
- she won the award for the best supporting role
- they don't know where you are
- down the street and over the bridge
- completed only months before
- when she ran across the line
- it's made of cotton
- shake the bottle well before you open it
- made from 100% cotton
- the lady who lives next door
- he found it on the floor behind the sofa
- she'll tell you how to make it

If you can tell which are sentences and which are not, by 'intuition', that's enough for the present. You can come back to it later with a bit more knowledge.

# Clauses and phrases

A **clause** is a group of words containing one finite verb (see page 22). It is often only a section of a sentence. Here is a sentence with two clauses.

You'll need to speak to the person/who arranges the timetables.

Together these clauses make a complete sentence. The first clause could be a sentence on its own, but the second couldn't unless we gave it an initial capital and a question mark.

Some sentences have only one clause.

He bought it this morning.

Some have more.

Old Alf revved the engine/and off they went towards the river mouth,/while we waited on the jetty/until they were out of sight.

A **phrase** is also a group of words. It is a looser structure than a clause. It is short, doesn't have a finite verb (it may not have a verb at all) but it functions as a kind of unit. Here are some examples:

- *under the table*
- *after the exams*
- *in the drawer*
- *hundreds of fish*
- *eating peanuts*
- *through the door*

We haven't got far, but at this stage we will leave clauses and phrases for a while, and look instead at words, the raw material of our communications. When we have tried to identify and classify words, we will be able to return with greater understanding to consider clauses in more detail, and to examine their different kinds.

# Words – and their functions

We classify words according to the work they do. If you've heard of **parts of speech**, it simply means classes of words, grouped according to function.

We will deal with them in the following order:

Nouns	the names of things
Pronouns	the _he me them_ words
Verbs	the action words
Adjectives	the describing words
Adverbs	the _how when where_ words
Prepositions	the _to in at_ words

And
    a
       few
          other
             bits
               and
                 pieces.

Now for a bit more detail (but not too much).

 # Nouns

A noun is the name of something: a thing or a person or a place, or even a feeling or a state of mind.

house   *Layla*   *delight*   *pencils*   *Paris*

There are **four kinds of nouns.**

Common nouns are the names of ordinary things we can see or touch:

house   *chicken*   *banana*   *boy*   *town*

Proper* nouns are the names of particular or special things or persons or places. In English they have an initial capital:

Adelaide   *Michael*   *Christmas*   *April*

Collective nouns are names for groups of things or people:

crowd   *class*   *flock*   *choir*   *fleet*

---

* Doesn't mean the rest are improper

Abstract nouns are the names of things we can't touch or 'put in a box'. We often use these ones without saying *a* or *an* or *the*:

pain   pleasure   beauty   wisdom   sunshine

Your teachers may talk about the **case** of nouns (and pronouns). They will mention nouns as being **subjects** and **objects** of verbs. We'll deal with the notion of grammatical case on page 17, in connection with pronouns, and again when we discuss verbs.

# Pronouns

Conversation would sound very strange if we had no pronouns. These are the words we use when we want to refer to people or things without continually repeating their names. If we really wanted to, we could say:

I saw Snoopy this morning. Snoopy came early to get Snoopy's books.

It's much more convenient to use some pronouns:

*I saw Snoopy this morning. **He** came early to get **his** books.*

Below is a table of **personal pronouns,** arranged according to 'person'. You will work out what 'person' means in grammar as you study the table.

Person	Subject pronouns	Object pronouns	Possessive pronouns	Reflexive or emphatic pronouns
First person singular	I	me	my, mine	myself
First person plural	we	us	our, ours	ourselves
Second person singular and plural	you	you	your, yours	yourself, yourselves
Third person singular	he she it	him her it	his, his her, hers its (with **no** apostrophe)	himself herself itself
Third person plural	they	them	their, theirs	themselves

A case of case

If you are learning another language, then depending on what it is, you may very soon hear about **case**. You will encounter it in relation to nouns and pronouns. Modern English doesn't worry very much about case, but we do have some vestiges of old cases in our pronouns, so we'll use them to illustrate.

When a small child says, 'Me like Timmy', we smile, knowing that the child will soon pick up the correct form and say, 'I like Timmy' (provided of course that Timmy remains in favour). In grammatical terms the child has made a mistake in case, using the object form **me** instead of the subject form **I**.

(With this in mind, think about the growing tendency to say things like, 'Her and her mother do the shopping together.' Would we say, 'Her does the shopping'?)

The table on the opposite page shows other forms for pronouns besides subject and object, but beyond these, English does very little in the matter of case. Some languages have different forms, usually shown by different word endings, not only for subject and object, but for other purposes as well.

The differing endings are called inflections, and English, over the centuries, has dropped most of its noun and pronoun inflections in favour of other ways of showing meaning.

As well as **personal pronouns**, there are also

RELATIVE PRONOUNS

>*who   whose   whom   which   that*

We use these in contexts such as

- *I've just met the man **who** designed it.*
- *Isn't that the boy **whose** story was on TV?*
- *The book **that** they really want is out of print.*

The relative pronoun **whom** is not very popular these days, but it may still be used in formal contexts.

- *To **whom** should we direct our complaint?*

We often omit **whom, which** and **that**

- *She's the one (whom) we want to see.*
- *Here are the cakes (which or that) you ordered.*

And there are

INTERROGATIVE PRONOUNS, the same words as the relative pronouns, but with different functions.

- *Whose* is this desk?
- *Which* cup do you want?

and **INDEFINITE PRONOUNS**

> *anyone   somebody   everything   etc.*

# Verbs

Verbs are the **doing, being, having** words. Their basic forms are the forms you find in the dictionary, and you can put **to** in front.

to eat   to write   to sing

The 'to' form is called the infinitive. It's the one they used to tell us not to split.

Verbs can be

one word
*He **finished** the work yesterday.*
*I **have** the tools you **want**.*
*This tea **is** awful!*

two words
*Sam **is coming**. (or Sam's **coming**)*
*Sam **is** not **coming**.*
*He **was running** round in circles.*
***Have** you **started** yet?*

three words
*I'll **be seeing** them later. (**will be seeing**)*
*That chapter **has been printed** already.*
*She **will have finished** by then.*

more than three
*By September they **will have been living** here for two years.*

Verbs and their subjects

Every finite verb has what is called a **subject**. That's the person or thing that does the action. It will be a noun or a pronoun, and in an English statement it comes before the verb. To find the subject of a verb, therefore, you simply need to ask yourself **Who?** or **What?** before the verb. Whodunnit! In the examples that follow, the subjects are circled and the verbs are underlined.

- *In 1987 (they) left the city.*
- *The (Mayor) drives a vintage Holden.*
- *(I) think (the train) arrives at three.*

In questions we either reverse the order:

- *Is (she) here?*
- *Were (you) sick this morning?*

or divide the verb into two parts, separated by the noun or pronoun that is the subject.

- *Did (they) go home?*
- *Do (the Johnsons) live here?*
- *Can (she) do it?*
- *Was (the cat) sleeping on your bed again?*

Finite verbs

We have already said that a finite verb has a subject, and that the subject is the doer of the action.

Look at the following sentence.

Thinking he heard a knock, he went out to check.

In this sentence there are four words that suggest action: **thinking**, **heard**, **went**, **check**. Are they all finite? We can eliminate **check** because it has **to** in front of it, so we already know it is an infinitive. Do the other three have clear subjects? We ask Who? or What? before each one. There is nothing at all before **thinking**, so we can eliminate it too.* That leaves **heard** and **went**. Who heard? Who went? Each of these is preceded by the pronoun **he**. So each has a subject and each is complete. Both, therefore, are finite.

---

* *thinking* is a participle. See page 30.

Verbs and their objects

As well as subjects, verbs often have **objects** (but not always). The object is the person or thing having the action done to it, so again it will be a noun or a pronoun. Look at two of our earlier sentences again.

- In 1987 they left the city.

  object of left

- The Mayor drives a vintage Holden.

  object of drives

More examples:

- Take the medicine every morning.

  object of take

- He forgot the directions and lost his way.

  object of forgot   *object of lost*

If a verb has an object it is called a transitive verb. If not, it's called an intransitive verb. (Predictable.)

The objects we have just looked at are **direct objects.** There are also **indirect objects.** They too will be either nouns or pronouns.

- *I gave her the letter.*

In this sentence *the letter* is the direct object, and *her* is the indirect object. You can work out the next three for yourself.

- *Then the officer asked me three questions.*
- *Did Sue give her mother the flowers?*
- *I'll tell you the answer later.*

Verbs active and verbs passive

Some verbs are said to be **active**. With active verbs the subject actually performs the action.

- *He arrived in an old blue truck.*
- *I hope she gets here soon.*
- *When will they be coming?*
- *They live in Oodnadatta.*
- *We were watching the news when Helen came.*

Some verbs are said to be **passive**. With passive verbs the subject has the action done to it. Isn't this a direct contradiction of what we said before? The sentences that follow should help.

- *The old blue truck was still driven regularly.*
- *Has the parcel been sent yet?*
- *These shoes were made in Brazil.*
- *All the documents will be shredded.*

We use both forms in everyday speech. Why the two forms? When do we use the passive form?

- When the action is more important than the doer.
  I'm afraid her arm has been broken.

- When we don't know the doer, or it doesn't matter.
  These shoes <u>were made</u> in Brazil.

- When we don't want to accuse anyone.
  My book's <u>been</u> torn.

- In wide-ranging general statements.
  Football <u>is played</u> all over the world.

- In public notices and formal documents.
  Trespassers <u>will be prosecuted</u>.

- In scientific writing.
  The test <u>was administered</u> three times.

Verbs and their tenses

Whichever language we speak we need some way of indicating when an action is done. Some languages, including English, do this by altering the forms of their verbs. We call these forms **tenses**, and the different verb-endings, like the different endings for nouns and pronouns, are called inflections.

Consider the following sets of sentences. For convenience we will use the pronoun **I** for the subject of the verb each time. You can work out the forms for the other subjects such as **she, we, they** and so on, if they differ.

- *I lived there ten years ago.*
- *I was living there at the time.*
- *I used to live there.*
- *I had lived there before I met her.*
- *I did live there.*

These are all ways of indicating something happening in **the past.**

What about **the present?**

- *I <u>live</u> there.*
- *I'm <u>living</u> there at present.*
- *I <u>do live</u> there.*
- *I <u>have lived</u> there.*
  (This 'past' has a present significance.)

What about **the future?**

- *One day I <u>will live</u> there.*
- *I'll <u>be living</u> there then.*
- *I'm <u>going to</u> live there next year.*
- *By December I <u>will have lived</u> there two years.*

Bigger grammar books will have names for all these verb forms, so you can look them up if you need to. Your target language may have a simpler verb system than English has, but if it does it will have other ways of showing time. On the other hand, it may have far more complex verbs than English has.

Regular verbs? Irregular verbs?

The verb **to live**, which we have just looked at, is a regular verb in English. Maybe you have never thought about bits of language being regular or irregular. But consider:

I live	*I lived*	*I have lived*
I help	*I helped*	*I have helped*
I consider	*I considered*	*I have considered*

These verbs are regular. They 'obey the rules'.

But

I write	*I wrote*	*I have written*
I eat	*I ate*	*I have eaten*
I sleep	*I slept*	*I have slept*
I drive	*I drove*	*I have driven*

These verbs are not at all regular. They go their own individual ways.

Participles

There are two other verb forms in English that you may find it useful to know about. They are called **participles**. There are **present** participles and **past** participles. **Present participles** are easy. They're the **-ing** forms.

Add **-ing** to any English verb and you have a present participle. Use a present participle along with *am*, *is*, *are*, *was*, *were*, *have been* etc. and you get the continuous tenses: *was going*, *are sailing*, *am trying* and the rest.

Past participles are less simple. The regular ones (see regular verbs, previous page) just take **-ed** as an ending, or **-d** if they already end in **e**. The irregular ones do their own thing, so we get *eaten*, *written*, *gone*, *driven*, *had*, *drawn* and scores of others.

Participles by themselves are not finite. We don't use them by themselves. We don't say, for instance, *he drawn, I eaten.* The fact that we do say, *he worked* and *they helped* simply shows that with regular verbs the past participle and the simple past tense are identical. You will learn to recognise them by their functions in context.

Auxiliaries

More jargon. Look at this sentence:

He will be staying there for three weeks.

The complete verb in the sentence is **will be staying.**
You already know that **staying** is a present participle.

The words **will** and **be** are called auxiliary verbs. In
primary school they used to be called helping verbs.
If you look back at other verbs we have discussed
you will recognise other auxiliaries, **have** and **am**
to name just two.

Most auxiliaries are also finite verbs in their own
right when they are used alone, but auxiliaries when
they are used in conjunction with participles.

Imperatives

These are the verbs for instructions and commands. They don't take different forms in English, but they may in other languages. There are two examples on page 8. Go back and look them up. (That's another example for you – two in fact.)

Here are some more:

- *Watch your step!*
- *Beat the butter and sugar together.*
- *Put your toys away, please.*
- *Take the next turn to the right.*

Direct and indirect (reported) speech

Have you ever noticed how we alter our verbs when we report what someone has said?

> *She said, 'I'm going to get a coffee.' The others said, 'We'll come too.'*

If we report this to someone else some time later, we'll say,

> *She said she was going to get a coffee. The others said they were going too.*

Try playing around with some more examples. You'll think of plenty.

# Adjectives

These are the words that describe things.

- *This possum's usual home is the wet forest.*
- *Why does she keep that rickety old bike?*
- *Are they clever?*
- *Oxygen is colourless, tasteless, odourless and abundant.*

Most adjectives are always adjectives. That is, we don't use them as verbs or nouns or anything else.

wild	*long*	*irregular*	*conscientious*
wide	*beautiful*	*expensive*	*cool*

But some adjectives look like verbs. In fact they are parts of verbs, but they do the work of adjectives.

an exciting story	*an excited child*
a boring lesson	*bored students*
a painted picture	*a writing implement*

Other adjectives look like nouns. They are nouns doing the work of adjectives. English has plenty of them.

- *Give him his account.* — noun
- *Here's the account book.* — adjective
- *Mine is a big family.* — noun
- *Our shop is a family concern.* — adjective

Look again at the first two sample sentences on the previous page.

This possum's usual home is the wet forest.

Why does she keep that rickety old bike?

This and **that** in such contexts are also considered to be adjectives. They are called demonstrative adjectives. Their plurals, of course, are **these** and **those**. Some grammars and dictionaries see these as articles (determiners). See page 42.

Comparison of adjectives

Sometimes we need to compare one thing with another – or even lots of things with others. We do it like this:

	cheap	cheaper	cheapest
	long	longer	longest
	happy	happier	happiest*
But	good	better	best
	bad	worse	worst

The -er form is called the **comparative**.
The -est form is called the **superlative**.

For longer words we say (for instance)

expensive	more expensive	most expensive
annoying	more annoying	most annoying
intelligible	more intelligible	most intelligible

---

* Note the spelling of this one. Other adjectives ending in -y follow the same pattern.

Adverbs

They used to say that adverbs tell how, when and where a thing is done. You'd expect, therefore, to find adverbs connected to verbs, and that's where they mostly are, not always alongside, but still connected.

'No', he said, and laughed loudly.

They come here often.

We've carefully planned all the moves.

Please arrive punctually.

There are adverbs of:

manner   *wisely   happily   clumsily   honestly*

well   fast   hard

Wisely, she locked the medicine chest.

Well done!

Don't hit it hard.

time   *yesterday*   *then*   *later*   *frequently*

Can you come *later?*

place   *here*   *there*   *down*   *somewhere*

Jack fell *down* *and broke his crown.*

degree   *quite*   *almost*   *very*

We're *almost* *ready.*

> *This adverb is connected not to the verb*
> *but to the adjective* <u>ready</u>.

Then there are adverbs for asking questions:

How?   *Why?*   *Where?*   *When?*

Where *was Jack going?* *Why* *did he fall down?*
And *how* *did he break his crown?*

There are comparative and superlative forms for
adverbs of manner, just as there are for adjectives.

wisely	*more wisely*	*most wisely*
happily	*more happily*	*most happily*
effectively	*more effectively*	*most effectively*

But   *well*   *better*   *best*

Prepositions

Here are all those words, usually little ones, like

to   in   at   from   by   before

which tell us how something is positioned or done in relation to something else. We use them for place, for time and in abstract ideas.

place	***in*** *Carmen's bag* ***behind*** *the tree* ***through*** *the window* ***on*** *your desk*
time	***before*** *three o'clock* ***in*** *September* ***during*** *the night* ***from*** *Monday* ***to*** *Thursday*
abstract	***in*** *tune* *a difference* ***to*** *your studies* *information* ***about*** *the program* *a third* ***of*** *the total*

Sometimes we can get a whole string of prepositional phrases in the one sentence, **separated by commas.**

> *Off went the pup <u>at</u> high speed, <u>out of</u> the room, <u>down</u> the stairs, <u>out</u> the door, <u>across</u> the garden and <u>into</u> the street, **with** Joey **after** him.*

Conjunctions

These are words that join ideas. The ideas may be single words . . .

> *yellow **and** blue*

or lengthy clauses:

> *I want to get there as early as possible*
> ***so** I'll take the 6:30 am train.*

Other common conjunctions are:

> *or   but   because   if*

Articles
(or determiners)

a   an   the   some   any   other   another
this   that   these   those   (and a few more)

Not all the grammarians agree about some of these, so you may find some dictionaries classify them differently. In traditional grammars **the** is known as the definite article, and **a** and **an** as the indefinite articles.

Some in this list have more than one function, so the dictionaries may give them more than one label. *This*, *that*, *these* and *those*, for instance, are also known as demonstrative adjectives, as you saw on page 35.

# Exclamations
(interjections)

Hey!

Wow!

Ouch!

Cool!

There's not much to say about these, but it is convenient to have a label for them.

✳ More about clauses

We've looked at nouns, and the work they do, and at adjectives and adverbs and the work they do. Let's go back now to clauses, and see how a whole clause can function like a noun or an adjective or an adverb. We'll start with **noun clauses**, since nouns were the first class of words we studied.

Noun clauses

We all know this policy is controversial.
(We all know **something**.)

She said she needed a new chair.
(She said **something**.)

That the old chair was falling apart was clear to everyone.
(**Something** was clear to everyone.)

Whether we go tomorrow depends largely on Jack.
(**Something** depends largely on Jack.)

These whole clauses function as nouns. You can put the word **something** in their place and it makes sense. It may not be brilliant sense, but it is sense.

Like a noun, a noun clause can be the subject of a verb. The noun clause in the third example is the subject of **was (clear)**. The one in the fourth example is the subject of **depends**.

Or it can be the object of a verb. The noun clause in the first example is the object of **know**. The one in the second example is the object of **said**.

Adjective clauses

An adjective, you recall, describes a noun. An adjective clause does the same. We saw some of these in the section on pronouns, because an adjective clause often starts with a relative pronoun such as **who**, **which**, **that** or **whom**. It would be a good idea at this stage to read that section again. It's on page 18.

Here are some more examples. The adjective clause is circled, and the arrow points to the noun described.

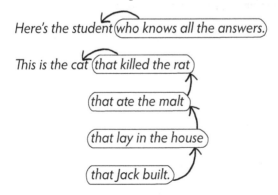

Here's the student (who knows all the answers.)

This is the cat (that killed the rat)

(that ate the malt)

(that lay in the house)

(that Jack built.)

He wrote a long report in which he detailed the whole experiment.

I consulted my grandmother, a lady in whom I have great confidence.

The visitor centre will have all the information you need.

As you can see, in the last example there is no relative pronoun introducing the adjective clause. It is omitted but 'understood', and it could be either **that** or **which**.

Adverb clauses

If English has plenty of adverbs, which you remember are words that mostly describe actions, why should we have whole clauses instead of single words? Sometimes there is no single adverb that says what we want to say, so we string together a clause to do the job.

There are adverb clauses of:

time
They came in <u>when the rain started</u>.

You'll be notified of changes <u>as they occur</u>.

place
I found my keys <u>where I put them yesterday</u>.

purpose/reason
We'll enlarge it <u>so that everyone can see</u>.

<u>Because we were going to be away</u> we asked the neighbours to collect our mail.

manner
He fled <u>as if the hounds were after him</u>.

condition
If it rains too much we'll cancel it.

concession
Holmes knows the answer, <u>though he isn't telling anyone</u>.

In conclusion . . .

Obviously this short guide barely scratches the surface of the subject of English grammar. You won't find anything here about modals, subjunctives, the past perfect tense, or even countable or uncountable nouns.

But if it helps you in your everyday pursuits, or in your efforts to learn another language, it will have achieved its aim.

If it stimulates you to want to know more about the structures and idiosyncrasies of English, then go to the experts who have written much more detailed volumes. There are plenty to choose from.

PART 2

Punctuation

Preface:
What this part
is and isn't.

Suddenly one day you have to produce something in writing. Is writing something you enjoy? Then you may not find it difficult.

But perhaps you really don't like writing at all, and you're faced with having to write something. A report? Some family history material? Minutes for a club or committee meeting? How will you deal with it?

Punctuation will actually help you to say what you want to say, and help you say it clearly. This section deals with everyday punctuation for everyday writing. In it you'll find the basics only. It's a no-frills approach. It will not give examples of rare or complex literary constructions needing complex punctuating, or detailed instructions for punctuating specialist material.

If you need specific instruction on such things as footnotes and end notes, referencing, bibliographies, mathematics and scientific writing, follow the instructions provided by your university or college.

Larger dictionaries and English style guides also give more detailed information on specific punctuation marks (see page 103).

# Intro

If we didn't already have a system of punctuation, someone would invent one.

> *The problem is that we have a perfectly good one but people don't know it – so they write or type a line or two – then have a vague feeling that there should be some sort of mark to indicate some sort of pause – so they do the first thing they can think of – and put in a quick shapeless pen stroke – or tap the hyphen key – and presto the thing is punctuated.*

But why not use the system we already have? It's there, it's simple, it's effective, and it's accurate.

We have all proved that we are quite capable of using very small signs accurately, and we do exactly that every time we type an email address or look up a website. We know we have to miss only one dot, or put a hyphen instead of an underscore, and either the email goes nowhere or we can't find the website.

If we can punctuate our emails, we can punctuate the rest of our writing – and that includes our advertising, our resumés and cover letters, our assignments, our social media posts. It includes everything we write.

Let's use the system we have. Let's use it now to deal with that indigestible mouthful at the top of the previous page.

> *The problem is that we have a perfectly good one, but people don't know it. They write or type a line or two, then have a vague feeling that there should be some sort of mark to indicate some sort of pause. So they do the first thing they can think of. They put in a quick shapeless pen stroke, or tap the hyphen key, and presto! The thing is punctuated.*

Punctuation isn't as difficult as you think it is.

I'm writing ordinary sentences. What punctuation marks do I need?

The beginnings of sentences seem to look after themselves. Just try to remember to start with a capital letter. It's the rest of the sentence that may need some thought. Sometimes it's hard to know whether to end it and start a new one, or to add further sections.

I'm just making statements, some short, some longer

That means you are saying something complete and definite. If your statement is short, then all you need is a **full stop** [.] at the end.

She always wants to ride her scooter to school.

You know he never reads newspapers.

All the chocolate ones went first.

I know.

If you want to put several items into the one sentence, you will still need a full stop at the end, but you'll need to put a mark, probably a comma, after each item or section.

I want to break up a long sentence

How do you decide when a sentence is finished? How do you know when to use a full stop and when to use a **comma** [,] or occasionally a **semicolon** [;]? Here are some sentences to consider, and then improve.

> *We met the three of them in a café soon after we arrived, we all had coffee together, they live out in the suburbs now, they just happened to be in town that day.*

It's a bit of a mess. It's not that the sentence is too long. The problem is that the pieces of information in it just seem to be piled in without any thought. It makes better sense and better writing to divide it according to the information it gives and the order in which things happen.

> *We met the three of them in a café soon after we arrived. They live out in the suburbs now, and just happened to be in town that day, so we all had coffee together.*

Here's another example.

> *Fifteen people came to the first meeting, we plan to meet every second month, the next meeting will be in May, we'll meet at Pat's place.*

Here's an improved version.

> *Fifteen people came to the first meeting, and we decided to meet every second month. The next meeting will be in May at Pat's place.*

You can work out the changes. Here's another example.

> *There's one more working bee this year, it's on 28 November, if you can help please let us know, there are lots of jobs to be done, morning tea will be provided.*

Let's improve it.

> *There's one more working bee this year, on 28 November, and there are lots of jobs to be done. If you can help, please let us know. Morning tea will be provided.*

We could call this the comma problem. It's not simply that we write long sentences and don't break them up. The problem is that we write a brief statement, think of something else to add to it, put a comma in and write the new bit, and then another comma and another new bit, and on we go. Then when it looks long enough and has enough commas (or hyphens or other vague marks) we end it with a full stop.

Instead, let's think about a logical sequence for the contents of the sentence, and be prepared to start a new one at a logical point.

There is more information about the use of commas in the section on inserting an extra thought into a sentence (page 60) and in the section on lists (page 91).

What are colons and semicolons?

Colons [:] are the marks you use to introduce a list of things. Read about them in the section on lists, which starts on page 91. **Semicolons** [;] are another way of dividing a sentence, or of joining two sentences. They aren't as popular as they used to be, but some authors still use them, usually to link two thoughts that are very closely related to each other.

Modern advertising doesn't only aim to inform us about new products and services; it aims to make us buy them.

He inherited quite a sum from his grandfather, but it wasn't enough to pay for a new place; they would have to wait a few more years and hope that prices didn't go up as steeply as they had that year.

Sometimes colons and semicolons are interchangeable; you could use either of them in both of the sentences just quoted (or in this one). If you want more specific information on semicolons, go to a more detailed authority, such as one of those listed at the end of this book. There is, however, one particular use of semicolons mentioned in this book, and you will find it in the section on lists (page 91).

I want to insert an extra thought into a sentence to make it clearer

If we want to use big words we can call these extra bits parenthetical insertions, and for most common purposes you can choose one of several ways of inserting them. There are **brackets** [( )], **dashes** [–] [—], which look like extra-long hyphens, and even the ordinary old **comma** [,]. Brackets themselves are often called **parentheses**. Here they are:

> He found his hammer **(**the one he'd been using all his working life**)** in the shed where he'd left it the day before.

> He found his hammer — the one he'd been using all his working life — in the shed where he'd left it the day before.

> He found his hammer – the one he'd been using all his working life – in the shed where he's left it the day before.

> He found his hammer**,** the one he'd been using all his working life**,** in the shed where he'd left it the day before.

There are two dashes to choose from. The shorter stroke is known as an **en rule** or **en dash** [–], and the longer one is known as an **em rule** or **em dash** [—]. When you use **dashes**, please use the short ones with a space either side as this is the preferred style in Australia. A **hyphen** [-] isn't big enough, and anyway hyphens have their own purposes (see page 64). To type an en dash in Microsoft Word, press option+hyphen key on a Mac. For desktop PC, press ctrl+minus on the numeric keypad. For PC-laptop, Microsoft Word automatically corrects a hyphen to an en dash if it has spaces on either side. So, you can insert an en dash by typing the required words or numbers with a spaced hyphen in between.

There are also **square brackets** [[ ]] for specialist contexts, such as commenting on quoted material by another writer. Square brackets are used in this book to enclose examples of punctuation marks. **Round brackets** [( )] (or parentheses) are often used in numbering, for example (23), 5(b), 10(iv).

I'm asking a question

All you need at the end of your sentence is a question mark [?].

Have you seen them?

Has he got the tickets?

Did you get your computer fixed?

Are you really going to the Grand Final, or are you just kidding?

Truly?

I want to shout, blow my stack, say something astonishing!

This is probably one situation for which you need no instruction. Use an **exclamation mark** [!].

It's true!

We've won!

I've told you a dozen times I've never met her!

But wait a moment. How often do you want to shout? The punctuation specialists are undecided on this one. Some say use exclamation marks as much as you like. Others suggest you limit them to one per page or email, and never use more than one at a time. Some say they are a bit like antibiotics, that the more you use them the less effect they have.

If you have been in the habit of using lots of exclamation marks, stringing them up like socks on a line, then maybe you could think about using them a little less often. Give yourself a challenge, and think how you could write something just as startling using words only.

What's the difference between a hyphen and a dash? Aren't they the same?

Let's see what the Macquarie Dictionary says:

hyphen a short stroke [-] used to connect the parts of a compound word divided for any purpose. (Macquarie goes on to tell us, 'Many compounds start out linked by a hyphen but as the compound form becomes more established there is a tendency for the hyphen to disappear.') Examples include bestseller, groundbreaking and wheelbarrow. It didn't take long for E-mail to become e-mail, then email.

dash a horizontal line [–] [—] used in writing and printing as a mark of punctuation to indicate an abrupt break or pause in a sentence, to begin and end a parenthetic clause . . . and for other purposes.

Macquarie also gives another definition for dash:

dash a hasty stroke, especially of a pen.

Hyphens and dashes are a misused lot, and too often get used where a comma should be used, or even where a sentence should really end. (Go back to the example at the top of page 53, and see if this is your problem.) In lots of casual writing, even when it's intended for printing or publication, the poor old hyphen, or something like it, seems to have become the all-purpose punctuation mark. Why did I put a hyphen in **all-purpose**? Because I wanted those two words to be linked very clearly, as described in the definition.

Think of the sentence you're trying to write. You have two words side by side that you think might need a hyphen. Read the sentence, maybe a few times, maybe aloud. Would a hyphen make the meaning clearer? If it would, use one. If not, let the words remain two words.

But there are situations that should always take hyphens:

- in double-barrelled words like *double-barrelled*, *by-product*, *self-help*, *gluten-free*, *vice-president*
- when a long word has to be divided at the end of a line. When you have to divide a word, put your hyphen between two syllables. For example, *intro-duction*, (not introdu-ction), *estab-lish* (not esta-blish, **and never, never anything like** *establi-sh*)

- in cases like *re-cover*, meaning 'cover again' as opposed to 'get over some illness'; and *re-mark*, meaning 'mark again' as opposed to 'speak out or comment'. In these cases the meaning is unclear without the hyphen
- in those contexts where you string several words together as if they really are to be considered one word, such as a *never-to-be-repeated experience*, *his wake-up-late morning*, *a not-for-profit enterprise*
- when you are writing double-barrelled numbers in words, for example *twenty-five*, *sixty-two*.

Here is an example of how **not** to use a hyphen:

This year will see bigger and better events for the festival-the 20th anniversary celebration!

In this example there is actually a new word. It's **festival-the**. Correct it by using an **en dash** [–] and get:

This year will see bigger and better events for the festival – the 20th anniversary celebration!

What about this example?

If it's chocolate-we have it.

Again, a new word has been created: chocolate-we. The sign writer has actually connected the very words that were meant to be clearly separated. Use an **en dash** instead:

If it's chocolate – we have it.

Or simply a comma:

If it's chocolate, we have it.

Here is a sentence that would be very much improved by the use of a few hyphens.

She says she's sick, but she just has first day of the week itis.

Where would you put the hyphens?

She says she's sick, but she just has first-day-of-the-week-itis.

Capital letters can be confusing. When should I use them? When shouldn't I use them?

Oh dear. Local advertisers and those who write public notices are using initial capitals all over the place, especially where they aren't needed, while others have just about stopped using them altogether.

Look at this advertisement.

Trade Courses Online. Creative, Student Focused, Varied, Comprehensive Instruction From Qualified and Experienced Teachers. Many Trades to Choose From.

Why all the unnecessary capitals? Are they for emphasis? Does the writer want to tell us that every word is very important?

Here's another. This notice was on a ferry. It had no punctuation at all.

*Please Do Not Leave Personal Belongings Unattended
The Crew Will Not Accept Responsibility For
Any Loss Or Damage*

What about:

Musicians
did you know?
You can Try, Buy
& Learn in the one Place!

What's wrong? Unnecessary capitals. There are
two sentences in this ad, and no personal names, so
only two capitals are needed, one at the beginning
of each sentence. A comma after **Musicians** would
improve it too.

But some advertisers have gone to the opposite
extreme. How about this one?

need insurance?
there are insurance experts just down the street.
us.
we're there for you.

Is the writer simply trying to show that advertisers
are above **all** the rules? With the rise of text
messaging, using capitals seemed to go out of
fashion for a while. These days, while the use
of capitals might be more relaxed when texting
friends, it's still best to use them in general –
especially in a professional setting.

Wouldn't it make more sense to write:

Need insurance?
There are insurance experts just down the street.
Us!
We're there for you.

Do we need capitals for the following items?

- Names of people **Yes**
  Tom, Dick, Clementine, Ms Brown

- Names of places **Yes**
  France, Victoria, Geraldton

- Names of groups of people **Yes**
  Turkish, Awabakal, Japanese

- Names of languages **Yes**
  Indonesian, German, Mandarin

- Names of everyday things **No**
  house, computer, cat

- Names of months and days **Yes**
  August, Monday, Anzac Day

- Street and road names **Yes**
  York Street, Oxley Highway, the name of your own street

- Special landmarks, buildings, etc. **Yes**
  the Sydney Harbour Bridge, the Eiffel Tower, the Great Barrier Reef

- Names of religions   *Yes*
  Christianity, Hinduism, Judaism

- Literature, music, art, films   *Yes and No*
  Usually capitals for the first word and the main words, small letters for the rest. Perhaps the best advice for book titles is to follow what is printed on the title page, or the page near it which gives publication details. Authors sometimes make their own decisions on this matter, and sometimes the designer or typesetter may have some influence.
  The House at Pooh Corner, The Secret River, The Moonlight Sonata, The Times Atlas of the World.

- Initials of organisations   *Yes*
  RSPCA, UNICEF, AFL

- Official personal titles   *Yes and No*
  Capitals for main words, lower case for the rest.
  the Mayor of Hobart, the Prime Minister of Australia, Sir Walter Raleigh

- Scientific names of plants and animals
  Yes and No
  The generic (first) name always has a capital,
  the specific (second) name doesn't. Both should
  always be in italics.
  Eucalyptus haemastoma, Mus musculus

- Names of people, places or trademarks that have
  become ordinary words   ***No***
  biro, laptop, velcro, bandaid, vegemite

- Words we want to emphasise   ***No, no, no***
  In print, use **bold** or *italics*. In handwriting,
  underline.

Catchy advertising that deliberately mimics kids'
handwriting and deliberately confuses capitals and
lower case letters doesn't help us! It doesn't help
children either.

Please! Please tell me about apostrophes.

When should I use them?

1. We use them to show that someone owns something

Usually an **apostrophe** ['] and an **s** are what you need. It's not even difficult to decide where to put the apostrophe.

I must take Jill's book back.
Jill owns the book.

He keeps an eye on William's house.
William owns the house.

The tall man over there is the child's father.
The child owns the father.

The city's new mayor is the youngest ever.

The city owns the mayor.

I got it straight from the horse's mouth.
The horse owns the mouth.

Where does the apostrophe come? After the owner.
(Perhaps not all these show actual ownership, but for this purpose we treat them as if they do.)

What if the owner is plural? Look at this passage.

> *We try to encourage gardening in this school. Here is the infants' section, over there is the primary boys' part, and the next one is the primary girls' section. I'm afraid the teachers' garden is still in the future.*

Where does the apostrophe come? After the owner (or in this case, owners).

Here's another poor example:

Parent and Teacher's Committee

What's wrong? Does this committee really only have one parent and one teacher? That's doubtful. To correct it, write:

Parents and Teachers' Committee

What about the words that have odd plurals? There is no problem with *kids* and *boys* and *gardens* (well, no punctuation problems). But what about *child*? *Lady*? *City*? *Man*? *Woman*? We make some changes and get *children, ladies, cities, men, women.*

Where do we put the apostrophe now? **After the owner again**. That gives us *children's, ladies', cities', men's* and *women's*.

Longer words that end in *y*, like *opportunity*, *identity* and the rest, seldom need to show ownership, and if they do we lengthen the whole thing, and write, for example, *the advantages of these opportunities*, rather than the clumsy *these opportunities' advantages*.

What about when two people own something? Do we add an apostrophe to each name? No. We put an apostrophe on the second.

Jack and Harry's dog became a favourite.

Do you know where Rick and Lupita's flat is?

So there seems to be one major rule, and it's easy to remember. **The apostrophe always follows the owner**. Check it out and see if it fits all cases. There may be an *s* after the apostrophe (children's) or there may not (cities') but the apostrophe always follows the owner. The only exception is *its*, and for that little exception, see page 80.

What about a word, or maybe a person's name, that ends in **s**? There may never be agreement on this one. Rules (and exceptions to them) have been made and changed more than once, but here is one suggestion for a solution. It may not please all the rule-makers, but it is a suggestion. Suppose you want to indicate that something is owned by Jess, or Luis, or Chris, or perhaps John Davis or Jenny Harris or Mr Coroneos, or anyone else whose name ends in **s**. Let's take a cricket bat owned by Thomas.

Try saying the thing aloud. Do you really feel comfortable saying *Thomas' bat*, (pronounced *Thomasbat*), giving a total of three syllables? Does *Thomas's bat* sound better (with four pronounced syllables?) If that's the way we say it, then it seems logical to write it that way.

Let's try a one-syllabled name. Do we say *Chris' book* (pronounced *Chrisbook*)? Or do we say *Chris's book*? If we say *Chris's book*, then let's write it that way.

If we follow this suggestion with given names, we can do it with surnames. So we will get *Phil Douglas's idea, Judy Burns's enterprise*, and even *Mr Trass's shop*. But doesn't *Trass's* give us a triple *s*? No. The apostrophe prevents that.

The suggestion here for dealing with names that end in **s** or **es** is simply, **If you pronounce it, then write it.** It may not cover all cases, but it may help.

For instance, you wouldn't write *the Lewis' live here*. The apostrophe in this case means nothing. And the correct plural for Lewis is *Lewises*. Spell the name the way you would pronounce it: *Lewises*. If we want to mention something owned by the Paderewski family (the Paderewskis) or the Jayawardena family (the Jayawardenas) or the Haynes family or the Wilkes family, we can always try to restructure the sentence and avoid the apostrophe problem by writing *the house where the Paderewski family lives*. We can even do this with the Haynes family and the Wilkes family, if we can't cope with the idea of saying *Hayneses* or *the Wilkeses* (both of which are acceptable).

Popular usage is winning out, as it always does eventually in language, so this small book doesn't give hard-and-fast rules for writing plural and possessive forms of people's names.

2. We use apostrophes to join words together to make a shorter form

Here is another use for apostrophes. When we want to write the way we speak, or when we want to write informally, we need to know how to write those shortened forms of common expressions that we use all the time in conversation: things like *I'm, she'll, won't, they're, he's, wouldn't* and all the rest.

What does the apostrophe do here? It shows we've left out a letter or two, in order to put on paper something that tries to mimic what we actually say. How do we decide what letters to omit?

Here are the conventional spellings of the common ones. Most of them are fairly predictable, even fairly logical.

I have > I've	*he is, he has > he's*
I had, I would > I'd	*she had, she would > she'd*
I am > I'm	
I will > I'll	*he will > he'll*
we have > we've	*they have > they've*
we had, we would > we'd	*they had, they would > they'd*
we are > we're	*they are > they're*
we will > we'll	*they will > they'll*
you have > you've	*it is > it's*
you had, you would > you'd	*it had, it would > it'd*
you are > you're	
you will > you'll	*it will > it'll*
will not > won't	*is not > isn't*
do not > don't	*was not > wasn't*
shall not > shan't	*were not > weren't*

cannot > can't	*are not > aren't*
must not > mustn't	*must have > must've*
should not > shouldn't	*should have > should've*
would not > wouldn't	*would have > would've*
could not > couldn't	*could have > could've*
have not > haven't	*had not > hadn't*
did not > didn't	

We can even say and write *wouldn't've, shouldn't've, couldn't've.*

But, what about this sentence?

> *The platoon had lost its commander and was surrounded.*

You notice that *its* has no apostrophe. Why? Did we forget it? No. **It doesn't need one.** We only use an apostrophe for **it's** when it means **it is.** And for that, go back to the previous page.

Its tells us that **it** owns something:

> *Look at the dog, still chewing **its** old bone.*

> *The new machine has **its** problems.*

It's means **it is:**

*Please, please tell me **it's** not true.*

***It's** not timber. **It's** only plastic.*

Government departments and government officials, especially those who decide on the content of public notices and signage, seem to have decided against apostrophes altogether. It has been said that they do this for clarity, that apostrophes clutter the signs. It is now decades since the apostrophes were deleted from place names such as Frenchs Forest, Delaneys Creek, Coxs River, St Helens.

It is sad that the authorities seem to have decided that punctuation generally is a bit of a chore. If you want to write clear English, don't follow their example.

When shouldn't I use them?

There's a big **don't** for apostrophes. Don't, please don't use them in plurals. Not even in names.

- five coffee's *No!* — five coffees *Yes*
- three taxi's *No!* — three taxis *Yes*
- four church's *No!* — four churches *Yes*
- canary's for sale *No!* — canaries for sale *Yes*
- a few comma's *No!* — a few commas *Yes*
- the Anderson's *No!* — the Andersons *Yes*
- two Ben's in the class *No!* — two Bens in the class *Yes*
- TV's, DVD's and CD's *No!* — TVs, DVDs and CDs *Yes*

There's also no need for an apostrophe in expressions like *the 90s*, or *the 1850s*, and if you write such expressions in words, then the spelling follows ordinary spelling patterns. Examples: *the forties, the nineties, the twenties.*

I'm quoting something written by someone else. What are the rules?

If you're quoting only a few words or a couple of lines, you can insert your quote straight into your own paragraph, enclosed in quotation marks (inverted commas). As with writing conversation, you can choose whether to use **double quote marks** ["] or **single quote marks** ['], but once you have made your choice, stick to it. It's wise to be consistent. Single quotes are generally preferred by publishers in Australia.

Are you writing an essay? The penalties for plagiarism are heavy. You will need to acknowledge the source, even for a short quote, and the best thing to do is to follow the rules provided by your education institution. These rules will probably be the ones agreed on internationally. If your quote is a whole paragraph or more, it is usual to indent the entire quote so that it is immediately visible and distinct from your main text. You may also decide to use a smaller type or even a different font or type style, like this:

If you're quoting only a few words or a couple of lines, you can insert your quote straight into your own paragraph, enclosed in quotation marks. As with writing conversation, you can choose whether to use double quote marks ["] or single ones ['], but once you have made your choice, stick to it. It's wise to be consistent.

I want to shorten the quote, but I still need it to read smoothly. How?

You can do this quite easily. Read carefully and choose words, phrases, or perhaps even a whole sentence that can be omitted without affecting the sense of the passage. Replace the omitted words with three dots called an **ellipsis** [...]. Your quote should now read as if nothing has been omitted. The omission can be from the middle of the sentence, or from either end.

Here is a sentence that could be shortened, and a suggestion for doing it.

> 'The feeling of mystery and great solemnity hanging over the ancient ruins adds to their attraction, indeed their enchantment.'

> 'The feeling of mystery . . . hanging over the ancient ruins adds to . . . their enchantment.'

There is another use for quote marks

Can't quite find the word you want? Know another one that's close, or suggestive, or related, or gives a hint? Or one that is a bit unusual? Perhaps it's a foreign word, or a bit of technical jargon, or even just a bit of humour. These examples might help.

> *Her student days were spent in a top-floor 'apartment', not much bigger than a large cupboard.*

> *Unfortunately the 'aid' wasn't very helpful.*

> *The 'library' was a small collection of books in a box in the storeroom.*

> *It was only a trickle down the slope, but for the children it was 'the waterfall'.*

How to misuse quote marks

Here are two places where inverted commas (quote marks) should **never, never be used**. They are not for emphasis, and they are not for decoration.

Here are some examples for you **not** to follow. Examples like these are common but not to be copied.

1. *Our cakes are 'baked daily'.*

The bakers evidently don't know that the marks they have used have their own meaning, and it isn't emphasis or decoration. What do the bakers mean? What they have printed in big letters outside the shop actually tells me that:

- The cakes *might* be baked daily.
- They bake their cakes daily and they want us to know it, and they think this is the way to say it.
- They really only pretend to bake their cakes daily, but they want us to think those cakes are fresh every day without fail.
- They don't really know what these marks mean but they think they look good.

2. *Get your 'live' worms here.*

I'd have some doubts about those worms. Are they really alive? Does the seller simply hope they are alive? Are they pretending to be alive? The shop keeper is trying to assure us that they are really alive and fresh and healthy and wriggling, but that's not what the notice says. The notice simply tells me that the seller wants to emphasise the freshness of the worms, but doesn't know how to do it.

3. *Our products are made of genuine 'recycled' plastic.*

Do the manufacturers know that they are actually saying almost the opposite of what they want to tell us? No doubt the plastic is genuinely recycled, but that is not what the message says. It says, 'Our products are not really made of genuine recycled plastic, but we want you to think they are'.

How could the writers of these messages have presented them so as to get their meaning across clearly and correctly? One answer for all three would be to leave them alone. Just leave them alone. Please, if you are in the habit of using quote marks as a way of emphasising something or making it stand out or just decorating it, stop. Quote marks are not meant for those purposes. There are other ways, agreed and accepted, for showing emphasis (see page 97).

4. *Joseph J. Bloggs, B.A. L.L.B.*
   'Accredited Specialist in Industrial Law'
   Expertise and Understanding

What's wrong here? It's an unnecessary (and wrong) use of inverted commas. This is not a conversation. Inverted commas are not for decoration, and they are not for emphasis. In this example, the inverted commas imply that Joseph J. Bloggs isn't really an

87

accredited specialist in industrial law. There are also four unnecessary capitals used. Here is the example, correctly punctuated:

Joseph J. Bloggs, B.A. L.L.B.
Accredited specialist in industrial law
Expertise and understanding

We could improve it further by making it into a sentence, so that the last three words aren't left hanging in mid-air, and take out unnecessary full stops:

Joseph J Bloggs, BA LLB
As an accredited specialist in industrial law,
I work with expertise and understanding.

✳ I want to write a conversation, just as it was spoken.

Not many of us are going to write novels or short stories, but maybe one day we'll want to record a dialogue. It could even be part of an assignment.

We have some choices here. We know about **quote marks** (or inverted commas or quotation marks). They have two uses. My computer has ['] and ["] on the same key. As mentioned earlier, Australian publishers generally prefer single quotes, so if you intend your work to be published, it would be as well to remember that.

If we simply want to report conversation the way we do when we are chatting, then we don't need any special marks.

> *Simon told the others he was going fishing. They said they'd go with him.*

If we want a label for this, it's known as reported speech or indirect speech. But if we want to record Simon's exact words (direct speech), we write,

Simon said, 'I'm going fishing.' The others said, 'We'll come with you.'

It doesn't matter whether you choose to use double quote marks or single ones. But you need to be consistent throughout the piece of writing, so once you've made your choice, stick to it. There's a reason for this. You may need to write a quotation that is actually inside another quotation – the quote within a quote, like this:

He stated in court, 'My father said, "Go home",
and I had to obey'.

Or if you choose to use double quote marks for the direct speech then the words of the father appear within single quote marks to make them stand out, like this:

He stated in court, "My father said, 'Go home',
and I had to obey".

# Lists.
Are there any rules?

Everyone makes lists. Some are a bit more formal than others. Is there a right way? Are there several right ways?

If it's your shopping list or a list of the things you want to do this week, there are no rules. Do as you have always done, on the back of an envelope or anywhere else.

But perhaps you're doing an assignment and you need to include a short list in a sentence. All you need are some **commas** [,] and a **full stop** [.].

Before long the firm had offices in Japan, Belgium, Finland, France and New Zealand.

They discussed issues such as foreign affairs, financial affairs, trade, justice, security, the environment, agriculture and labour.

Notice that in these sentences you don't need a **colon** [:] after **in** or **as**.

Maybe you have to compile some facts in note form. You have data that isn't in sentences, and you don't need to present it in sentences, so you can do it with a colon, then commas.

> *Offices: Japan, Belgium, Finland, France, New Zealand.*

> *Issues discussed: foreign affairs, financial affairs, trade, justice, security, the environment, agriculture and labour.*

Perhaps your list contains items that all consist of several words. Here is where **semicolons** [;] will help, by clearly marking off the groups of words.

> *The recent Guide describes the history of the area; its most important industries and products; its local government; its social structure and institutions; its education system; and its hopes for the future.*

If your list is a lengthy one, it may be better to set it out in columns.

> *Offices now exist in:*

Japan	*South Africa*
Belgium	*Denmark*
Finland	*Canada*
France	*Kenya*
New Zealand	*Brazil*

So far these examples are simply lists with no suggestion that one item is any more important than any other item. Occasionally, however, you need to show items in order of importance, or maybe in chronological order. You can do this in more than one way, but the choice is still yours.

1. Japan	a) Japan
2. Belgium	b) Belgium
3. Finland	c) Finland
4. France	d) France
5. New Zealand	e) New Zealand

What about bullets?

Bullets [•] are especially helpful if each item is not just one word, but a phrase or a statement. If all the items in your list are equally important and you simply need to list them, bullets are probably the most common way these days, though some writers prefer **asterisks** [*] or other marks. You don't need a punctuation mark at the end of each item, but you should use one after the last item since it ends the sentence.

The committee needs to discuss:

- *trees along the boundary fence*
- *restoration of the old formal garden*
- *a possible fish pond*
- *replacement of old fruit trees*
- *general maintenance*
- *a possible date for starting*
- *recruitment of volunteers.*

Each item in the bullet list should make a complete sentence when you say it with the lead-in statement. The best way to check this is to read each item in the list as if it is part of the lead-in statement.

(The committee needs to discuss) trees along the boundary fence.

(The committee needs to discuss) restoration of the old formal garden.

And so on.

It's also a good idea to make sure that each item in the list is constructed in the same way. For instance, don't make one bullet point a question and the others statements. Be consistent.

Not strictly punctuation, but . . .

Is there a correct way to present dates?

We see them printed in a surprising number of different ways. Here is a selection of styles, all used by Australian newspapers. Notice not only the words and figures, but also the presence or absence of commas, and the use of capitals.

August 4, 2023

4 August 2023

FRIDAY AUGUST 4 2023

FRIDAY, AUGUST 4, 2023

friday august 4

Friday, August 4, 2023

Friday August 04, 2023

All of these use the full forms of day and month. Then there are the ones that abbreviate the names of the days and months, so we can add those to the list. And there is the form we see printed on our emails: *Friday, 4 August 2023*, and the one that appears on the email screen: *04/08/2023*.

We also see:

4.8.23

4/8/23

4-8-23

04.08.23

This set of options covers most of the Australian scene, so it should give us plenty of scope. If we go to Europe or America we find differences in the order of the items in the date. We may find:

day > month > year

year > month > day

month > day > year

and sometimes these forms come into Australia too.

None of the forms quoted here, incidentally, is the pattern that our grandparents, or even perhaps our parents, were taught at school. In my primary school that pattern was *Friday 4th August, 2023*, and the *th* may or may not have been superscript, as the computer now seems to prefer.

The best advice seems to be simply to choose one pattern and make it your habit. One day, perhaps, there might again be a way of writing dates that most people in most places agree on. For the time being, take your pick. But stick to it, at least within the one piece of writing.

How do I emphasise a word, or maybe several?

Are you writing an advertisement? Or a notice for a notice board? Please, please don't use quotation marks (inverted commas) for the bits you want to emphasise! Use a bigger typeface, or a different one, or use colour, anything but inverted commas. Please.

Are you writing by hand? Then <u>underlining</u> is the easiest, and is always understood. The only other common use for underlining in handwriting is probably the occasional heading.

In typed and printed material you can choose between *italics* and **bold**. You might even use ***colour***. Since there are some other contexts in which it is conventional to use italics, it may be best to decide on bold for emphasis, and make that your rule. For example:

> It wasn't **you** I was thinking of, it was **him**.

> We **had** to do it. We had no choice.

We use italics in the middle of 'normal' text when we want to mention the titles of books, poetry, plays and films.

Won't my spellchecker tell me when I've made a punctuation mistake?

Your computer puts a wiggly line under something you've typed, green for language, red for spelling. What's wrong? Spelling sometimes involves apostrophes, which is why the matter is mentioned here. Is the computer telling you you're wrong? Or is it just asking you to check? Is it saying, for instance, 'Do you really want an apostrophe here?' Is it suggesting that you would be better off choosing a different word?

Don't automatically think you've made a mistake. The computer is not always correct. Sometimes it will suggest something that makes you doubt what you have written, even when you haven't made any mistake. On the other hand, sometimes it will fail to query something that really is wrong.

One day I deliberately typed: *That's wonderful new's!*

The computer was happy with *That's* (because it is correct) but of course *new's* got a wavy line under it, so I consulted the spellchecker. It gave me five suggestions, and none of them worked. It is difficult to imagine a context in which any of them would be correct. It should have told me simply to omit the apostrophe, and all would have been well. Here are the spellchecker's suggestions: *news's newt's mew's now's net's.*

Here are some more.

I typed: *We need two new dictionarys.* The spellchecker suggested *dictionaries* (correct), *dictionary's* (could perhaps very occasionally be correct), *dictionary* (the word is spelt correctly but is not the right word for this context)

I typed: *The warning appear's regularly*. The spellchecker suggested *appeal's, paper's, appears* (correct).

Here is a short item, containing an error, that wasn't questioned at all:

The babies crying.

This is wrong but the spellchecker accepted it because *babies* is a word, just not the correct one for this sentence.

Note that the spellchecker doesn't know the difference between words that sound the same but are spelt differently, such as *for, four* and *fore; in* and *inn; wait* and *weight*. Also most, if not all, spellchecker programs use American spelling and American punctuation rules. You can usually change the settings to Australian spelling.

What are the correct short forms for words like gram, litre, metre?

This list contains only those words that are commonly wrongly abbreviated. The internationally accepted forms are as follows:

gram	g
kilogram	kg
metre	m
kilometre	km
centimetre	cm
litre	L (this one is a capital because the lower case is too easily mistaken for a capital I)

You don't need to put a full stop after any of these, and you don't need to add **s** for plural. So you get:

five grams	5 g
a hundred kilometres	100 km
twelve litres	12 L

# In conclusion . . .

So there you have it. Punctuating your writing, in order to make it clearer and easier to read, is a sensible thing to do, and it's really not difficult.

The basic rules are simple, and if you start to take care, they will very soon become automatic. You will find yourself punctuating your work correctly without even thinking about it. It's worth trying.

# Helpful books

Most of the larger dictionaries have instructions and information on punctuation, usually at the back of the book. Particularly helpful are:

The Macquarie Dictionary

The Concise Oxford Dictionary

Also very informative and helpful is *The Australian Government Style Manual*, which can be accessed online.

Printed in the USA
CPSIA information can be obtained
at www.ICGtesting.com
BVHW040411140823
668485BV00001B/9